FRANZ SCHUBERT

TRIO

for Piano, Violin and Violoncello
E♭ major / Es-Dur / Mi♭ majeur
D 929

T0084440

Ernst Eulenburg Ltd

London · Mainz · Madrid · New York · Paris · Tokyo · Toronto · Zürich

Trio

I.

Franz Schubert, Op. 100
1798-1828

E. E. 1185

Ernst Eulenburg Ltd

19

E. E. 1185

II.

Andante con moto

Un poco più lento

III.

Scherzo Allegro moderato

Fine

38

E. E. 1185

40

Scherzo D.C.

IV

Allegro moderato

L'istesso tempo

51

85-4*   E.E.1185

55

E. E. 1185

E.E. 1185

L'istesso tempo

64